The Ultimate Baby Shower Guide

The Ultimate Baby Shower Guide

Shayna Andrews

Writers Club Press

San Jose New York Lincoln Shanghai

The Ultimate Baby Shower Guide

Writers Club Press
an imprint of iUniverse.com, Inc.

For information address:
iUniverse.com, Inc.
5220 S 16th, Ste. 200
Lincoln, NE 68512
www.iuniverse.com

All scripture is from the New International Version unless otherwise noted.

ISBN: 0-595-18335-2

Printed in the United States of America

DEDICATION

Lord, I dedicate this book to you. It was through you that I conceived the vision of what this book will be and it is the first of many to come. I never imagined you would lead me down the road of an author. You have empowered me to prosper and have given me the treasures of darkness, riches stored up in secret places. Thank You, Father, for the covenant you made with Abraham—a covenant of prosperity, perfect health and perfect peace—and that I am heir to that covenant through faith in Jesus Christ according to your word in Galatians 3:14. Thank You for taking my right hand and opening doors before me that no man can close. All nations on earth that hear of all the good things You do for me will be in awe and tremble at the abundant prosperity and peace You provide me. Through me and my descendants the peoples of the earth will be blessed. I thank You, Father, that no weapon formed against me shall prosper. I am blessed coming in and going out and everything I put my hand to prospers. I have favor among men. Thank You, Father, that not one of all Your good promises fails. Every one is fulfilled. Lead me, Lord, in your righteousness and make straight your way before me. You have filled my heart with greater joy. Thank You, Jesus, for fixing your eyes on me, the joy set before you, so that you could endure the cross. Thank You, Holy Spirit, for ministering to the hearts of the people who read this book and bringing people to a relationship with Jesus. I love You, Lord.

CONTENTS

PREFACE

This book began as I was helping to plan a baby shower for a friend at church. In fact it was the fifth baby shower that year. I wanted it to be different than the others. How many showers have we attended and it was the same thing? The same games, the same food, the same thing! I realized that often times it is one person within a group of friends that plans the baby showers and it is the same group of women that attend each one. I wanted to create a resource that someone could use more than once and have a completely different shower the second, third and every shower after that. A shower that would be unique to the person it is being given for and fun and interesting for the guests who attend.

I trust that you will find the inspiration you are looking for to create a perfectly unique shower for your guest of honor. I hope that your shower is all that you dreamed it to be.

ACKNOWLEDGEMENTS

Thank you to my friends, Maura, Angela, Melissa, Marcia, Jessie and Becky, who allowed me to photograph their beautiful babies. Thank you to Mom, Gwynne Thompson, Tammy Carnes, Tina LaBlanc, Socorro Armendariz, Maria Duran, Jessie Rubio and Alma Santa Cruz for allowing me to print your family recipes. You are awesome women of God. You have been anointed and equipped to preach the good news and minister to the broken hearted. You will be richly rewarded! Thanks Eric for your invaluable professional advice. I appreciate your friendship. The Lord has big plans for you! I look forward to seeing those things come to pass in your life.

I love you!
Shayna

INTRODUCTION

Having a baby is a wonderfully exciting time in a family's life. Hosting a shower for the parents-to-be is a fantastic way to celebrate the arrival of a new baby and show your love for the parents-to-be.

Unfortunately, there are many teens and young women getting pregnant and because of the unexpectedness of the pregnancy, they are not able to enjoy this special time. Do not hesitate to host a shower for a young mother because other people view the pregnancy as a mistake. Instead, take this opportunity to show her how much she is loved regardless of the choices she has made and let her know that God has a purpose for her and her baby. Jeremiah 1:5 says, "Before I formed you in the womb I knew you." And Psalms 139:13-14 says, "…you knit me together in my mother's womb…I am fearfully and wonderfully made…". This is the time to build her up and encourage her. Prepare her for what is to come. Tell her she does not have to fail because she is young. Proverbs 16:3—"Commit to the Lord whatever you do and your plans will succeed." Let her know you are there to lean on when things are uncertain.

Every child is worth celebrating. Having a shower for the second, third, fourth or fifth baby is just as significant as a shower for the first-born. Remember, showers offer friends and family the opportunity to supply the family with all the necessities of parenting that child.

THE BASICS

Isabel Symonne
3 years

He must acknowledge the firstborn by giving him double share of all he has.

Deuteronomy 21:17

Showers are no longer boxed in by traditional styles. Anything you can dream up is appropriate for today's baby showers. Whatever type of shower you decide to have, remember that it is for the whole family and in many instances, the father-to-be would like to be included. So, as you begin to plan your shower, find out from the guests of honor their preferences and plan around them.

Generally, a close friend or relative hosts the shower. If you are the grandmother-to-be and you want to host the shower, go for it! This day is just as special for you. Children's children are a crown to the aged. Proverbs 17:6.

Some of the responsibilities you, as the host, will have are choosing a date, a location, the games, the theme, what food to serve, offering gift ideas to guests, and recording the gifts received at the shower. You will also need to delegate to someone to take pictures and/or run the video camera. Or, have disposable cameras laying on the tables and ask guests to take pictures throughout the shower.

1

As host, the most important thing to remember is that this is the mom's day. Shower her with love and attention and keep the focus on her.

Choose a Date

A shower held two—three months before the due date is generally enough time for the parents-to-be to get the nursery in order and make any purchases for items they did not receive. However, if you are hosting the shower in another state and the mother-to-be must travel, having the shower 3 months before the due date may make the travel more comfortable and help ensure there is no early delivery. Parents who decide not to know the sex of the baby before birth may prefer a shower after the "birth-date". This allows guests to choose gifts that are perfectly suited for the baby.

The Guest List

Be sure to ask the guest of honor whom she would like to invite and then you may add from there. Besides inviting close family and friends, you may want to include extended family, childhood or school friends, co-workers, or church friends. Inviting people from different aspects of the mother-to-be's life will be a wonderful surprise for her and a fun way for everyone who knows her to come together. Keep your budget in mind when making your guest list. If you want to keep everything under $200, do not invite fifty people. Ask how the mother-to-be feels about the size of the shower. Having fifty people there may be overwhelming to her or having only ten people may be too boring. Maybe she and the father-to-be would prefer a co-ed shower. Co-ed showers are becoming more and more popular and are a lot of fun. Always remember to keep her preferences in mind. You are guaranteed success when you do!

Invitations

As you prepare the invitations, keep these things in mind. The invitation should say whom the shower is for and who is hosting the shower. Include the date, time and location. If you know the sex of the baby, with certainty, include that with the due date. If the mother has registered, include the name of the store. Do not forget an RSVP name and number. Remember to save one invitation for the baby book, too.

Invitations should be sent out three weeks in advance and RSVP's should be in two weeks before the shower.

Choose a Location

Some ideas on where to hold the shower are at a home, a restaurant, a banquet room, church or a park. Wherever you choose, be sure it will accommodate your guests and offer privacy and intimacy. You do not want guests spread out and distant from each other. If you have the shower at a restaurant, make sure there are facilities and make reservations in advance especially if you choose a hot, new, trendy restaurant. Always confirm reservations one week before. If you decide to have the shower at someone's home, be sure to acknowledge their hospitality during the shower and offer a small gift to show your appreciation.

The Big Day

Most showers will last two—three hours. Of course, depending on the group you have it can go longer or shorter. Usually, a shower will begin by greeting guests and serving foods. Once all the guests have arrived, begin playing your games. Two to four games will be sufficient. Choose a variety of games. This way you are sure to have something that appeals to everyone. After the games, serve the dessert and have the mother-to-be open her gifts. Once the gifts are opened, guests will leave a few at a time. Make sure the guest-of-honor has the opportunity to say good-bye to everyone. As host, thank each guest for coming. If you have a favor for them, this would be the time to give it to them.

Get Organized

As host of the shower, it is very important that you are organized and prepared. This is a moment that will be forever remembered by the mother-to-be, good or bad. Take the time to plan out the shower so it is something that is fun for all. You should have just as much fun at the shower as your guests.

You may also be asked for gift ideas. If the mother-to-be has registered, enclose a registry card with the invitation. This will take the guess work out of the gift buying. If the mother-to-be is unable or not interested in registering, then you need to find out from her what she would like. She may have all the basics and just needs clothing. Maybe this is her second child but has passed down everything and is starting over. Use the "Gift Idea" worksheet to help her assess what items she will need. Have her check off what she would like and how many and you can use it to give to guests as they ask for ideas.

Copy and use to your advantage the following worksheets to help you get and stay organized. Being prepared and organized will make room for you to enjoy yourself as well.

Budget Worksheet

Items	Budget Cost	Actual Cost	Deposit Req.	Deposit Due Date	Date Paid	Balance Due	Balance Due Date	Date Paid
Banquet Room								
Party Rentals								
Invitations								
Flowers								
Decorations								
Tableware								
Food								
Cake								
Games								
Prizes								
Favors								
Gift								

Guest List Worksheet

Date and Time		Send Invitations By	
Name		Name	
Address		Address	
Phone	RSVP Yes / No	Phone	RSVP Yes / No
Name		Name	
Address		Address	
Phone	RSVP Yes / No	Phone	RSVP Yes / No
Name		Name	
Address		Address	
Phone	RSVP Yes / No	Phone	RSVP Yes / No
Name		Name	
Address		Address	
Phone	RSVP Yes / No	Phone	RSVP Yes / No
Name		Name	
Address		Address	
Phone	RSVP Yes / No	Phone	RSVP Yes / No
Name		Name	
Address		Address	
Phone	RSVP Yes / No	Phone	RSVP Yes / No
Name		Name	
Address		Address	
Phone	RSVP Yes / No	Phone	RSVP Yes / No

Shower Supply List

v	Item	Store
	Table Settings	
	Plates / Cups / Utensils	
	Napkins	
	Serving Pieces and Utensils	
	Punch Bowl and Ladle	
	Table Cloth	
	Decorations	
	Balloons	
	Wall Decorations	
	Gift Table Decorations	
	Cake Table Decorations	
	Yard Decorations	
	Centerpiece	
	Food	
	Cake / Dessert	
	Appetizers / Finger Foods	
	Mints, Nuts, Candies	
	Fruit	
	Vegetables	
	Snack Foods	
	Lunch	
	Punch Bowl and Ladle	
	Soda, Tea, Coffee	
	Miscellaneous	
	Invitations	
	Gift for Mother-to-be	
	Wrapping Paper	
	Card	
	Flowers	
	Prizes	
	Favors	
	Pens, Pencils, Paper	
	Paper Towels	
	Toilet Paper	
	Trash Bags	
	Hand Soap	
	Hand Towels	
	Chairs	
	Sing in Book	
	Camera, Film, Video Camera	

Gift Giving Worksheet

Name	Gift Description	Thank you

Gift Ideas

QTY	Maternity Clothes	QTY	Diapering	QTY	Nursery Items
	Blouses		Cloth Diapers		Crib
	Pants / Shorts		All-In-One Diapers		Bassinet / Cradle
	Dresses		Diaper Covers		Bassinet Liner
	Skirts		Diaper Service		Mattress
	Slip		Disposable Diapers		Mattress Pads
	Leggings		Wipes		Changing Table
	Panties / Bras		Wipe Warmer		Changing Table Pad
	Breastfeeding		*Bathing*		Rocking Chair
	Breast Pump		Bathtub / Bath Seat		Ottoman
	Storage Bags		Hooded Towels		Lamp
	Nursing Pads		Wash Cloths		Nightlight
	Nipple Cream		Baby Shampoo		Mobile
	Nursing Pillow		Baby Soap		Hamper
	Privacy Shawl		Baby Lotion		Wastebasket
	Books		Nail Clippers		Crib Blankets
	Pregnancy Journal		Baby Nail Files		3 pc. Crib Set
	Calendar		Rubbing Alcohol		Crib Sheets
	For Baby		*Travel*		Dust Ruffle
	Bodysuits		Diaper Bag		Waterproof Lap Pads
	Undershirts		Insulated Cooler		Play Yard
	Rompers		Bottle Warmer		*Bottle Feeding*
	Sleepers		Infant Car Seat		Infant Formula
	Socks / Booties		Infant Carrier		4 oz Bottles
	Mittens		Sling / Carrier		8 oz Bottles
	Caps		Stroller		Bottle Brush
	Receiving Blankets		Car Sun Shade		Nipple Brush
	Burp Cloths		*Toys*		Sterilizer
	Laundry		Swing		Bottle Warmer
	Laundry Basket		Floor Gym		*Other*
	Baby Detergent		Bouncer		Head Support
	Stain Remover		Developmental Toys		Feeding set
	Safety Items		Stuffed Animals		High Chair
	Monitor		Bath Toys		
	Thermometer		Books		
	Outlet Covers		Crib Toys		
	Gate		Walker		
	Nasal Aspirator		Tape Player		
	Humidifier		Cassettes		

CHOOSE A THEME

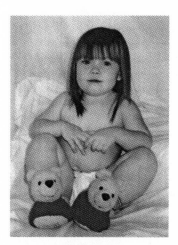

Sara Rae

23 months

The promise is for you and jour children and for all who ire far off – for all whom the Lord our God will call.

Acts 2:39

Themes will add character and individuality to your shower. A theme will also meet a specific need for the mother-to-be whether this is her first child or her fifth. A themed party does not have to be costly or time consuming to be successful. The most important factor is to make sure you inform your guests of the theme and what role they will need to play. Will they need to bring a particular type of gift? Will they need to be dressed in a particular style? Choose one of the themes below or use them to come up with your own ideas. Your shower is sure to be a hit!

Essential

This is great for the first time mother who needs all of the basics. Make sure the mother-to-be is registered at a local store so guests purchase the specific items mom needs.

Educational

Guests bring toys, books, videos, etc. that will aid in baby's development. A variation to this is for guests to bring a gift they have chosen but instead of a card, a book is enclosed.

Safety

Some mothers-to-be receive many baby necessities that are passed down from friends and family. If the mother-to-be has most items, why not have a safety shower? All the guests bring gifts that will help provide a safe environment. Examples are wall plugs, play yard, cabinet locks, books, etc....

Precious Moments

Celebrate the precious moments in mom and baby's lives. Instruct guests to bring gifts that represent baby's first words, foods, steps, photos, etc. Choose games that honor those precious moments. Decorate with Precious Moments.

Tea Party

This is a great idea for showers that have guests of all ages. Guests can dress up, enjoy teacakes, scones and a variety of teas. Decorate with dollhouses and doll furniture. For hostesses with a larger budget, why not hold the shower at a tea room?

Around the Clock

This is a fun shower! On each invitation, write a specific time of day. Guests bring gifts that would be useful for the time of day written on her invitation. For example, 2:00am = She could bring something like teething gel or diapers, 6:00pm = She could bring bibs or feeding items, etc.

Basket Shower

Have guests bring gifts that are all gift baskets. On each invitation write a different type of gift basket to bring. One could be a mealtime, bedtime, bath time, playtime, in the car, at Grandma's, etc. This shower is especially fun during the gift openings because each of the guest's gifts is unique and creative.

Coed

Make the men more comfortable at a baby shower and turn it into a BBQ. Choose games that are fun to do in teams. Good games to choose would be Baby Pictionary, Baby Relay, Diaper Changing Contest, Treasure Hunt, etc. and have a battle of the sexes. Stay clear of frilly games and decorations. On the invitations, make known that the shower is for both mom and dad and address both people as equal guests.

Previously Owned

Do you know somebody who is having multiples and is in need of double or triple of everything? There are many children's resale stores that carry good quality, barely used merchandise at a great discount. This will allow your guests to purchase more for their dollar. Some of these stores may also offer a registry service or a wish list. Some mothers may not be comfortable with used merchandise. Be sure to find out how she feels about it before you plan this type of shower.

Potluck

To help keep costs down for the hostess, host a potluck shower. This is wonderful for guests who already know each other and it creates a comfortable, informal atmosphere.

For All Seasons

For a mother-to-be who really enjoys nature, host a shower for all seasons. Have guests bring gifts that will be useful during the different seasons of the first year of baby's life. Gifts can be clothes, blankets, pool toys, snow gear, outdoor items, etc. When you assign the different seasons, be sure to include what age the baby will be during that season. This will help to make sure guests purchase age appropriate toys and properly fitting clothes.

Candid Camera

Stroll down memory lane with videos and pictures of the mom-to-be's childhood. The hostess will need to get together with the grandmother-to-be and go through family home videos. Edit tapes with funny clips from different times in the mom-to-be's life and show the video during the shower. Decorate with pictures of the mom-to-be. This is a fun shower for the mom-to-be and her childhood friends.

Long Distance Shower

When the mother-to-be lives away from family and friends and is unable to travel, you can still have a shower. Videotape the guests bringing gifts, playing games, and having cake. Or if both parties have computers, purchase inexpensive video cameras and the mother-to-be can interact with the guests in real time. Choose activities that will be keepsakes for the mother-to-be like making scrapbook pages or decorate t-shirts for the baby.

Collective Shower

This is for a mom who needs only large items or specific items. On the invitation explain the specific need of the mom-to-be and when the collection will be. Each guest makes a donation into the gift and the hostess purchases the items and presents the gifts at the shower.

Tacky Tea Party

If you are concerned about guests not knowing each other, break the ice before they even arrive by hosting a "Tacky Tea Party". Guests come dressed as tackily as possible and each brings a very tacky gift along with an appropriate gift. The house can be decorated with hanging pantyhose, trash left out, cluttered counters, etc. This shower is sure to be fun!

Match the Nursery

Find out from the guest of honor how she plans to decorate the nursery and instruct guests to purchase gifts that fall within the colors and theme of the nursery. Decorate the party within the same theme.

Big Sister / Brother

Make the new big brother or sister feel special. Theme the party by marking this milestone in his or her life. Big brother or sister can create banners and decorations for the party. Have guests bring a gift for the new baby as well as a small token for big brother or sister that will help aid in his or her new responsibilities.

Disposable Shower

For the mom who has everything, host a "Disposable Shower". This is a shower where all of the gifts are items that are disposable. For example, diapers, wipes, medicines, nursing pads, bottle liners, diaper pail liners, bath products, lotion, sunscreen, phone cards, etc. Encourage guests to use their imaginations.

Baby Clothing

For moms who have had a girl and now are expecting a boy (or vice versa) or for a mother of multiples, a clothing shower would be a great way to help out. Guests can purchase clothing in sizes from newborn—18 months. Tables can be decorated with little shoes and little onesies or sweaters can be hung on the walls or on a clothesline.

Mother's Shower

Get friends and family together to pamper the mother-to-be with a foot massage, facial and manicure & pedicure. This is a great idea for a mom-to-be who is already supplied with baby items or who is expecting multiples and will not have the luxury of time once the babies come.

Casserole Shower

Each guest brings a dish brought in a freezer/oven/serving container she does not want back attached with a recipe card. The idea is to provide the family with several prepared, homemade meals for the days when mom is unable to prepare a meal herself. This shower may be best to host closer to the due date.

Surprise Shower for Grandma

For moms who have the necessities, why not have a shower for the grandma-to-be? Guests bring gifts that Grandma will need when the baby is visiting. This is especially helpful when trips to Grandma's house will be overnighters.

Office Shower

Showers at the workplace can be a lot of fun but it is important to stay within the guidelines. Here are some tips to help you have a successful office baby shower.

- ❖ Ask for help from 2 or 3 other coworkers to divide up the tasks.
- ❖ Get approval from your supervisor if you are planning to hold it in the office.
- ❖ Verify with the mother-to-be's supervisor that she will be available at the planned time.
- ❖ Try to hold the shower during lunchtime when it is easiest for employees to take a break.
- ❖ Keep the shower to one hour.
- ❖ If the shower is being held in the office, have co-workers contribute an appetizer or salad, etc. or take up a collection.
- ❖ Guests can purchase their own gift or contribute to one large gift.
- ❖ It is not mandatory that people participate so be very casual when approaching co-workers for contributions.
- ❖ If collections are low, consider just serving cake on festive party plates.
- ❖ If you are unsure of what the mother-to-be needs, consider taking a collection for a gift certificate to a local store.
- ❖ If you decide to hold the shower at a restaurant, make reservations 2 weeks in advance. Confirm with the restaurant one week prior.

❖ Most office showers are too short on time to play games. If you do choose to play, keep it short and simple and more traditional than one you would choose for a shower at home.

❖ Keep decorations simple. There is not much time for set up and clean up. Use appropriate party goods and a bouquet of balloons. That will help to set the mood.

❖ Alcohol is inappropriate in an office setting.

THE DECORATIONS

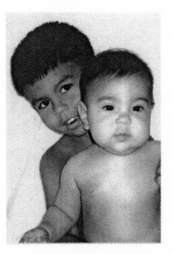

Christian Alexander
4 years
&
Layna Alexandra
6 months

Sons are a heritage from the Lord,
children a reward from him.

Psalms 127:3

Create a festive atmosphere by choosing decorations and tableware that reflect the personality of the family and the mood of the shower. Baby showers no longer have to be decorated with pink or blue streamers and balloons. Party supply stores and discount department stores offer a wide variety of options to choose from. Use your creativity! If you know that a family has a particular interest or hobby, decorate with that in mind. Many of the decorating ideas below can be used for many different décors. Read through each one and decide how it might fit into your party. Use the ideas to help you brainstorm and come up with a décor that is perfectly suited for the family you are hosting a shower for. Keep in mind to choose colors and paper goods that reflect the décor you have chosen

❖ Seasons—Decorate around things that are reminiscent of a particular season. It does not have to be the season the baby is due. If you live somewhere where winter is dreadfully cold and long and you are looking forward to spring, then celebrate springtime now. Have fun with it!
  o Fall
    • Decorate with dried leaves, pumpkins, and cornucopias. Think of the harvest time and Thanksgiving.

  o Winter
    • Use Christmas or New Year's decorations.

  o Spring
    • Think flowers, outings, enjoying Mother Nature.

  o Summer
    • Summer is a time for picnics, Independence Day, pool parties, and vacations.

❖ Family Ethnicity—Celebrate the family's heritage (Mexican, Hawaiian, Chinese, Indian, etc…) by including customs, decorations, traditional foods, etc. at the shower.

❖ Angels / Babies / Storks
  o Hang diapers on a clothesline and write one letter on each diaper to spell out "Baby Shower" or the baby's name.

  o Decorate with dollhouses and furniture.

  o Fill crocheted baby booties with candies or nuts.

❖ Clowns
  ◦ Baby toiletries can be used as weights for helium filled balloons.

  ◦ Bring in a balloon artist or do a little face painting to entertain guests' children.

  ◦ Decorate with bold, bright colors and blocks.

❖ Nautical / Sea Life
  ◦ Use a cute baby bathtub as a punch bowl. Fill it with a clear punch and let a sailboat float in it.

  ◦ Make seashell centerpieces.

❖ Gardening
  ◦ Make tiny topiaries in colors of pink, blue, white, yellow and green. Attach small baby items as ornaments.

  ◦ Group three or five baby bottles together and use them as flower vases. Set them around the cake or food table. Use different size bottles to add interest.

  ◦ Use fresh flowers on the cake.

  ◦ Group different size birdhouses together for centerpieces.

❖ Pooh Bear / Classic Pooh / Disney / Baby Looney Tunes
  ◦ If the mother-to-be has chosen the theme for the nursery, purchase an item to go in the nursery and use it as a centerpiece.

❖ Holidays
  ○ For Christmas or New Year's, hang tule and twinkle lights to make swags around the room.

  ○ If you are hosting during the Christmas holiday, decorate small Christmas trees with blue and pink lights and hang baby items as ornaments.

  ○ Make a baby wreath. Purchase a pre-made green or straw wreath and decorate with baby items and pink or blue ribbon.

❖ Teddy Bears / Animals
  ○ Decorate with stuffed animals.

  ○ Put Barrels of Monkeys on the tables as fun, interactive center-pieces.

❖ Noah's Ark
  ○ Decorate using a rainbow balloon arch and hang light blue curly ribbon from each balloon to simulate rain. Put the rainbow behind the cake or gift table that has a blue tablecloth.

  ○ Instead of nuts and candies, have a tray of frosted animal shaped cookies. Use the same cookies to create centerpieces. Stand three of the cookies up and frost the edges together.

  ○ Animal crackers are a great party favor.

  ○ Instead of cake, make cupcakes and decorate them with animal cookies or plastic animals.

Below are ideas that would dress up any décor you choose.

❖ For candlelight, put votives in baby food jars.

❖ String "It's a boy" and "It's a girl" confetti on the tables.

❖ Use the crib or stroller to display the gifts rather than the standard gift table.

❖ Fill a baby bathtub with individually wrapped toiletries. Partly blow up small balloons and place them in the tub as bubbles.

❖ Pacifiers and baby keys can be used as napkin rings.

❖ Small baby bottles can be filled with condiments for the sandwiches.

❖ Use room dividers to make a large room more intimate. Hang sweaters, booties, onesies, etc. on the screens to create interesting wall decorations.

❖ Fold a napkin in half and then into the shape of a diaper with a small pin in front. Dip the diaper into melted wax and shape it into a bowl. Use the diaper to hold nuts and candies.

❖ Decorate with a family heirloom.

❖ Decorate using classic children's toys like blocks, trains, or legos.

SERVING GREAT FOOD

Food is an important part of the shower but it does not have to be elaborate or expensive to be impressive. Food that is appetizing and well displayed is the most important factor to consider when planning this aspect of the shower. You do not need to be a gourmet to have a successful luncheon. These recipes are tried and tested and have been given to me by friends and family. Many of the recipes can be done ahead of time so you can spend more of your time enjoying the shower. You can put together an entire Mexican or Italian feast or simply serve a lovely dessert. Remember to keep in mind the time of day of the shower and plan your menu accordingly. Bon appetit!

Dips and Sauces

Tina's Artichoke Dip

1/2 c. frozen chopped spinach, thawed
1 c. chopped artichoke hearts, canned
8 oz. cream cheese or reduced fat cream cheese
1/2 c. grated parmesean cheese
1/2 tsp crushed red pepper flakes
1/4 tsp salt
1/8 tsp each onion and garlic powder
Dash of pepper

Boil vegetables in 1 cup of water for approx. 10 minutes. Drain. Microwave cream cheese for 1 minute. Mix all ingredients together. Serve warm in a hollowed out sourdough loaf.

Tina's BBQ Sauce

1 c. vinegar
1 c. catsup
1/2 c. dark corn syrup
2 tsp brown sugar
1/2 tsp each of salt, pepper, garlic powder, onion powder, tabasco sauce, and soy sauce

Mix all ingredients in a saucepan over medium heat for approx. 20 minutes. For thicker sauce, heat longer. For thinner sauce add a splash of vinegar.

Bean Dip

1 large can of refried beans
1/2 jar of salsa, approx. 1 cup
1 lb. Velveeta, cubed
1 tsp each of onion powder, garlic powder, red pepper, paprika, and chili powder

Mix all ingredients in a saucepan over medium heat, stirring until cheese melts.

Jessie's Salsa

6 small tomatoes
3 fresh jalapenos
1/2 tsp pepper
1 teaspoon salt
Pinch of garlic powder
Cilantro, to taste

Boil tomatoes and jalapenos together until the skin on the tomatoes cracks and is easy to peel. Drain. Peel tomatoes and pulse in a blender for a few seconds. Remove tomatoes and set aside. Place cilantro and peppers in blender and pulse for a few seconds. Add all ingredients together and stir.

Fruit Dip

8 oz. cream cheese
1/2 jar of marshmallow cream
1/2 c. orange, apple or pineapple juice

Mix all ingredients together. Chill. Serve with fruit tray.

Finger Foods

Fruit Tray

Strawberries
Watermelon
Grapes
Kiwi
Raspberries
Orange wedges
Cantaloupe
Bananas

Slice and cube fruit. Arrange fruit on a serving platter. Serve with Fruit Dip.

Vegetable Tray

Carrot sticks
Cauliflower
Broccoli
Celery
Cherry tomatoes

Arrange vegetables on a serving platter. Serve with a ranch dressing.

Tropical Fruit Platter

3 fresh pineapple slices, unpeeled, cut into wedges
2 kiwi, peeled and sliced
2 oranges, unpeeled, sliced, halved
1 papaya, peeled, seeded, cut into wedges
1 star fruit, sliced
1/2 lb. red grapes, clustered
1 banana, peeled, sliced
2 tbs fresh lime juice
1/2 c. frozen pineapple juice concentrate, thawed
1/4 c. coconut

On a large serving platter, arrange pineapple, kiwi, oranges, papaya, star fruit and grapes. Toss banana with lime juice. Drain, reserving juice. Arrange bananas over fruit on platter. In a small bowl, combine reserved lime juice and pineapple juice. Drizzle over fruit. Sprinkle with coconut.

Tina's Deviled Eggs

1 dozen hard-boiled eggs
3 tbs mustard
1/4 c. mayonnaise
1/4 c. miracle whip
1/2 tsp each of onion powder, garlic powder and paprika
1/4 tsp salt
3 pieces of crumbled bacon

Cut eggs in half and drop yokes into a bowl. Place the egg whites on a plate. Mix all of the ingredients EXCEPT paprika in a bowl on low speed until well mixed. Pipe or spoon yoke mixture into the egg whites. Sprinkle with paprika.

Tortilla Roll Ups

Flour tortillas
Cream cheese, softened
Green onions, sliced
Ham or turkey, sliced deli thin

Mix cream cheese and green onions. Spread mixture on one side of a tortilla. Top with ham or turkey. Roll up tortilla and slice. Serve chilled.

BBQ Meatballs

1 lb. hamburger
1 c. bread crumbs
Dash of pepper
1/2 c. milk
1 tsp salt

Mix all of the ingredients well and form into 1 inch balls. Put meatballs in a baking dish. Prepare BBQ Sauce and pour over meatballs. Bake 350° for 50 minutes.

Quesadillas

8 flour tortillas
1/2 c. sour cream
1/2 c. each monterey jack and cheddar cheese, shredded
Diced cooked chicken
Chopped tomatoes
Sliced mushrooms
Diced onion
Diced bell pepper

Spread 1 tbs sour cream over entire tortilla. Sprinkle with chicken, tomatoes, mushrooms, onions, bell pepper and cheese. Fold tortilla in half and press together. Place tortilla in a medium hot skillet. Cook for 2 minutes on each side or until golden brown. Remove from heat and set aside. Cook remaining tortillas. Cut into wedges.

Cheese and Crackers

Cheddar cheese
Monterey jack cheese
Swiss cheese
Variety of crackers

Slice cheeses to fit on crackers. Arrange cheese and crackers on a serving platter.

Garlic Bread

1 loaf of French bread
1 bulb elephant garlic

Roast entire bulb with skin on for 45 minutes in 300° oven. Remove and cool for 10 minutes. Cut off the top of the bulb and squeeze the garlic out. Spread over slices of bread and toast. If you do not have a toaster oven, place bread in the broiler and watch very carefully.

Salads and Side Dishes

Green Salad

Romaine lettuce
Red leaf lettuce
Sliced green onions
Sliced mushrooms
Chopped tomatoes
Chopped bell peppers
Chopped broccoli
Fresh cut corn from the cob
Chopped avocado
Chopped, fresh cilantro
Croutons
Crushed black pepper
Lemon

Mix all vegetables. Top with cilantro, pepper, and croutons. Squeeze fresh lemon over the top. Toss and serve.

Spinach Salad

1/2 lb. fresh baby spinach leaves
1 large can artichoke hearts, drained and sliced
1/2 c. black olives, whole
1 red pepper, diced
1 c. cooked chicken, shredded
1/2 c. shredded Parmesan cheese
Italian dressing

Place first 5 ingredients in a bowl. Toss with Italian dressing and sprinkle with Parmesan cheese.

Cucumber Salad

6 medium cucumbers, peeled and sliced
1 stalk celery, diced
2 bunches green onions, sliced
1 large tomato, chopped
1 bottle Italian dressing
1/2 c. apple cider vinegar
1 c. olive oil
1/2 c. sugar

Combine cucumbers, celery, onion and tomatoes in a bowl. Whisk together dressing, vinegar, oil and sugar. Pour over salad. Serve chilled.

Mom's Fruit Salad

Honeydew, cantaloupe and watermelon balls
Blueberries
Strawberries
Pineapple
Other fruits of choice

Mix all fruits together. Chill 2 hours before serving.

Jessie's Potato Salad

8 large potatoes
4 large eggs
1 can of black olives
8 oz. of mayonnaise
Mustard, enough to add yellow tint to salad
Salt
Pepper

Cut potatoes in half and boil 20 minutes with the skin on. Add eggs and boil another 10 minutes. Drain. Peel eggs and potatoes and place in a large mixing bowl. Add olives, mayo, mustard, salt and pepper. Stir. Chill before serving.

Sweet Potato Salad

4 large sweet potatoes
2 large potatoes
1 large red onion, sliced thin
2 eggs, hard-boiled
1 1/3 c. mayonnaise

Cut potatoes into quarters and boil for 30 minutes or until done. Drain and peel. Place potatoes, onion, eggs and mayonnaise in a large bowl and stir. Put in refrigerator for several hours before serving.

Macaroni Salad

1/4 c. mayonnaise
2 tbs lemon juice
2 c. cooked elbow macaroni
1 bunch green onions, sliced
1/2 c. artichoke hearts, drained and chopped
3 tbs fresh basil, chopped

Add first 3 ingredients. Stir. Add remaining ingredients. Stir well. Chill. If salad is too dry, add 1 tbs of mayonnaise at a time until desired creaminess.

Pasta Salad

1 lb. Rigatoni, cooked
1/4 c. fresh basil, chopped
2 cloves garlic, minced
3 large tomatoes, diced
1/2 c. black olives
2 tbs olive oil

Mix all ingredients in a large mixing bowl. Serve chilled or warm.

Socorro's Spanish Rice

Oil
1 c. rice
1/4 onion, chopped
1 clove garlic
Salt to taste
2 c. water and V8 or tomato juice, optional
(Do not add more than 2 cups of liquid.)
1 tsp chicken bullion, optional

Put oil in skillet. Wait until oil is hot then add rice. Stir constantly until it is slightly browned. Add onion and garlic. Next, stir and add the liquid, bullion and salt. Bring to a boil. Cover and put over a low heat until done. If it is a little dry, add a small amount of water.

Alma's Beans

2 c. of beans
salt to taste

Clean beans, rinsing them three times. Fill a large pot with water and bring to a boil. When it has come to a boil, add the beans. Bring to a boil. Cover and reduce to medium-low heat. Cook 1 1/2 hours. Add salt and cook for another 1/2 hour or until done.

Mashed Potatoes

4 medium unpeeled potatoes
1/3 c. skim milk
1/4 c. plain yogurt
2 tbs butter
1/4 tsp salt
1/8 tsp pepper

Cook potatoes in boiling water for 30 minutes. Drain. Combine all ingredients in a large mixing bowl. Beat on medium speed until smooth.

For a unique twist on an old favorite, use blue potatoes. Blue potatoes can be found in tropical areas or in specialty stores, when in season.

Sandwiches and Main Dishes

Hawaiian Chicken Salad

4 c. cooked chicken, shredded
1 1/2 c. sour cream
1/2 c. chutney, chopped
1 tsp curry powder
1/4 tsp ginger
1/4 c. shredded coconut

Combine all ingredients. Serve over lettuce leaves or in melon or papaya that has been halved and seeded.

Tuna Salad

4 cans water packed tuna, drained
1 large apple, diced
2 stalks of celery, diced
1/2 red onion, diced
2/3 c. mayonnaise or miracle whip

Mix all ingredients together and chill. Serve on whole wheat bread.

Gwynne's Egg Salad

12 eggs, hard-boiled, peeled, chopped
1/4 c. mayonnaise
2 heaping tbs hot dog relish
Onions, finely chopped
Celery, finely chopped
Olives, sliced
Vinegar, to taste
Sugar, to taste

Mix all ingredients together EXCEPT the eggs. Add eggs and stir.

❖ For a simple and easy alternative to finger sandwiches, take an unsliced loaf of bread and cut it lengthwise into 3 pieces. Spread egg, chicken, or tuna salad on one piece and a different spread on the 2nd piece. Top with the 3rd piece of bread. Soften some cream cheese and spread the cream cheese over the whole loaf. Cut into slices and serve.

Deli Sandwiches

Ham
Turkey
Roast Beef
Swiss Cheese
Muenster Cheese
Croissants or Dinner Rolls

Have the deli slice meats and cheeses very thinly. Roll each piece of meat and cheese and place on a platter. Cut croissants or dinner rolls in half and place in a basket next to the meat and cheese tray. Serve condiments in small bowls next to meat tray.

Heart Shaped Rolls

16 oz. hot roll mix
Vegetable spray
Herbs, to taste

Prepare mix, as directed up to shaping the rolls, adding herbs to your taste. Spray single serving heart shaped cake pans with vegetable spray. Divide dough into 6 equal pieces. Flatten and press into the bottom of pan going up the sides a little. Let rest until double in size, approx. 30 minutes. Bake for 15—20 minutes at 375°. When cool, cut in half. For smaller rolls, use a heart shaped muffin pan. Or for variety, use 6 different single serve pans or choose one that will fit with your theme or décor.

Quiche

1 onion, chopped
1 tbs olive oil
10 oz. frozen chopped spinach, thawed, pressed dry
5 eggs, beaten
3 c. cheddar cheese, shredded
1/4 tsp salt
1/8 tsp pepper

Sautee onion in oil in a large skillet until tender. Add spinach and cook until excess moisture evaporates. Combine eggs, cheese, salt and pepper. Add spinach mixture. Pour into greased 9 inch pie plate. Bake at 350° for 30 minutes or until set. To serve individual quiches, pour mixture into greased muffin pans.

Spinach Pesto Pizza

3 c. fresh, baby spinach leaves, torn
2 tbs. olive oil
1/2 c. parmesan cheese
2 cloves garlic, minced
1 red onion, sliced
1 pizza crust
1/2 c. black olives, sliced
4 oz shredded mozzerella cheese
1 c. cooked chicked, diced
1 c. chopped tomatoes
1 c. mushrooms, sliced
Italian seasoning

Sprinkle Italian seasoning over the pizza crust. Place spinach, olive oil, parmesan cheese and garlic in food processor or blender until smooth. Spread pesto over entire crust. Top with onion, olives, chicken, tomatoes, mushrooms and cheese. Bake at 400° for 20 minutes.

Lasagna

1 box lasagna noodles
16 oz. ricotta cheese
1 pkg. sliced mozzarella cheese
1 pkg. shredded mozzarella cheese
1 lb. ground sirloin, browned
15 oz. marinara sauce
1 tbs sugar
Sautéed onions, bell peppers, mushrooms, optional

Boil noodles according to directions, adding oil to the water to prevent noodles from sticking. When almost done, remove from heat and drain most of the water. Add marinara sauce and vegetables to the browned meat. Add sugar. Set aside. Baste 9x11 glass dish with butter. Lay noodles in pan. Next, spoon on ricotta cheese. Be sure to completely cover the top of the noodles. Then, cut 2 slices of mozzarella cheese in half and lay the 4 pieces on the noodles. The next layer is the meat sauce. Top with a layer of shredded mozzarella. Repeat. Bake for 30-40 minutes at 350º.

Alma's Enchiladas

8 oz. bag red chile
2 cloves garlic
Salt to taste
Dash of cumin, optional
Water
2 dozen corn tortillas
Oil
Cheese, shredded

Remove the seeds and the stem from the chiles. Rinse. Put chiles in a large pot with boiling water. Cover. Remove from heat and let them steam for 20 minutes. Drain. Put chiles in a blender. Add garlic, water, salt and cumin. Blend until smooth. Pour mixture through a sieve so that the liquid is smooth. Throw away what is left in the sieve. In a pot, pour a little oil and then the chile liquid. Boil.

In a skillet, pour oil to fry the tortillas until cooked to your preference. Place cooked tortillas onto a paper towel to absorb excess oil. Dip tortillas into chile sauce. Put a handful of cheese in the middle of the tortilla. Roll and place in baking pan. Repeat with remaining tortillas. Pour remaining sauce over enchiladas. Sprinkle top with cheese. Bake 350° until cheese is melted.

Desserts

Tammy's Cake Ideas

Purchase and prepare your favorite cake mix. Make it something special and unique with one of these fillings and/or frostings.

Banana Crème Filling

Instant banana pudding, prepared
Bananas, sliced

Lay bananas on the bottom layer of the cake. Top with pudding. Add top layer of cake and frost.

Fruit Filling

Peach, strawberry, raspberry or other fruit preserves.

Spread preserves over the bottom layer of the cake. Add top layer of cake and frost.

Fruity Crème Filling

Instant vanilla pudding, prepared
Favorite fruit preserves

Mix ingredients together and spread over bottom layer of cake. Add top layer of cake and frost.

Fruity Whip Crème Filling

Favorite fruit on the bottom yogurt
Cool whip

Mix ingredients together and spread over bottom layer of cake. Add top layer of cake and frost.

Shayna's Favorite Frosting

4 oz. of pudding
12 oz. cool whip

Stir together dry pudding mix and cool whip. Use chocolate, coconut, banana, vanilla or other puddings for a variety of frostings.

Maria's Rice Pudding

1 c. rice
2 c. water
2 sticks of cinnamon
1 can condensed milk
1/4 c. milk
Raisins, pecans, lemon zest, optional

Cook rice with the cinnamon sticks according to directions. When rice is cooked, add milk and condensed milk. Stir constantly until it comes to a boil. Remove from heat. Add optional ingredients.

Baked Bananas

4 bananas
1/2 c. brown sugar, packed
1/4 c. orange juice
3 tbs sherry
1/2 c. macadamia nuts
2 tbs butter
Dash of nutmeg

Peel bananas and place in a small baking dish. Mix next 3 ingredients together and pour over. Sautee nuts in butter then sprinkle over bananas. Add nutmeg to taste. Bake at 350° for 15 minutes or until tender and lightly glazed.

Chocolate Bowls

1 box of waffle cups
1 bar each of milk chocolate and white chocolate

Melt chocolates in separate bowls. Brush on chocolate, covering the inside and outside of each cup. Fill with candies, custard, fruit, mousse, parfait, etc.

Parfait

Chocolate or vanilla wafers
Your favorite flavor yogurt or pudding, prepared
Raisins, fruit, candies, cool whip, optional

Layer pudding, wafers and candies. Begin with pudding and end with a final layer of pudding. Top with a dollup of cool whip.

White Chocolate Mousse

Single serve graham crusts
1 bar white chocolate
1 can sweetened condensed milk
1/2 tsp vanilla extract
1 pint whipping cream

Put chocolate and milk in saucepan over low heat until chocolate is melted. Add vanilla. Cool and set aside. Beat whipping cream until stiff. Fold into chocolate mixture. Spoon into crusts. Chill until set, several hours. Garnish with fresh fruit.

Fruit Tart

Pre-made pie crust
Fresh fruit, sliced and prepared
8 oz. cream cheese softened
1/2 tsp sugar
1/4 c. fresh lemon juice
1/2 tbs each of grated lemon peel and orange peel.

Cook pie crust according to directions. Mix last 4 ingredients together and spread onto the bottom of cooked pie crust. Top with fruit.

Layered Pound Cake

1 prepared pound cake
2/3 c. strawberry syrup, divided
1-2 quarts vanilla ice cream, softened
3 c. fresh strawberries, sliced
1/2 c. whipping cream
1/3 c. strawberry syrup

Slice pound cake into 3 pieces, lengthwise. Spoon 2 tbs of strawberry syrup over 2 pieces of cake. Place bottom slice on a plate and spread 1/2 of the ice cream over it. Top with the middle slice and spread remaining ice cream over it. Top with the top layer of cake. Freeze until firm. Stir together remaining strawberry syrup and sliced strawberries. Set aside. Beat whipping cream and 1/3 c. strawberry syrup until stiff. Use immediately or refrigerate. To serve, slice cake and top with whipped cream and strawberry slices.

Fruit Topped Pound Cake

1 prepared pound cake
Sliced bananas
Sliced strawberries
Chocolate syrup
Cool whip

Slice pound cake. Add bananas and strawberries to each slice. Drizzle chocolate and top with cool whip.

Chocolate Raspberry Hearts

Pre-made pie crusts
1 bar milk chocolate
Fresh raspberries
Powdered sugar

Roll pie crusts out into a large circle. Using a heart shaped cookie cutter, cut pie crusts. Cook hearts according to directions for pie crust. Melt chocolate in a plastic zip lock bag in the microwave in 30 second intervals, being careful not to over cook the chocolate. Cut corner of bag and pipe chocolate over hearts and top with berries. Sprinkle with powdered sugar.

Carmel Apples

Tart apples
Bag of caramels
Popsicle sticks
Your choice of chopped nuts

Put popsicle sticks into apples. Melt caramels in a saucepan over medium-low heat. Dip apples into caramel. Roll apples into chopped nuts. Place on cookie sheet covered with wax paper. Chill.

Brownie Pizza

Your favorite brownie mix or recipe
Various toppings—
Pecans, walnuts, milk chocolate chips, white chocolate chips, peanut butter chips, broken candy bar pieces

Prepare brownies as directed. Pour batter into a pizza pan or a 13 X 9 pan. Cook according to directions. While still hot, place a different topping over each "slice" of the brownie.

Jell-O Jigglers

Use the Jell-O Jiggler recipe and pour into candy molds. You can find candy molds in the shapes of bottles, rattles, blocks, umbrellas, etc.

Beverages

Helpful Hint

Reserve some punch to make ice cubes. Pour liquid into ice cube trays. Drop 1 berry into each cube. Freeze. This will prevent your punch from getting watered down as the shower progresses.

Strawberry Lemonade Spritzer

1/2 gallon water
3/4 c. sugar
2 c. frozen strawberries
3/4 c. freshly squeezed lemon juice

Mix all ingredients together and let flavors blend for a couple of hours. If making in advance use fewer berries. If serving right away, use more berries.

Orange and Raspberry Punch

1/2 gallon orange juice
1/2 gallon vanilla ice cream or frozen yogurt.
3 c. frozen raspberries

Mix first 2 ingredients together then add the raspberries.

Horchata

1 c. long grain rice
4 c. milk
1/2 c. sugar
1 tsp vanilla
1/2 tsp cinnamon
Ice

Place the rice in a bowl with enough hot water to cover. Let the rice sit overnight. Next day, remove the water. Place 1/2 cup of water, rice and 2 cups milk in a blender. Blend until rice is all ground up. Mix in 1/4 cup sugar, 1/2 tsp vanilla, 1/4 tsp cinnamon. Do the same with the other half of the ingredients. Strain through cheesecloth. Serve over ice.

Citrus Spritzer

2 liter bottle of ginger ale
4 lemons
2 oranges
2 limes
Sugar to taste

Squeeze juice from fruit. Remove seeds. Add to ginger ale. Add sugar to taste. Garnish with sliced lemons and oranges.

BABY SHOWER GAMES

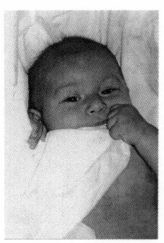

Sasha Sarai
5 months

A good man leaves an inheritance for his children's children.

Proverbs 13:22

Games are a great way to keep a party moving, especially when there are people who do not know each other! It is also a fun way for guests to be involved. Typically, two—four games are played depending on the length of each game. The showers of silly, embarrassing games have passed and now games have become more creative and more fun!

The games have been broken down into three categories: Games to Break the Ice, Games for the More Conservative Guests and Games for the More Adventurous Guests. Choose games that the guest of honor is comfortable with and are appropriate for the guests who will be attending. For example, if there will be several older people, do not choose a relay. Many of the games below are great for co-ed showers as well as all girl showers. Allow the guests to choose to participate. Someone may be uncomfortable with a particular game. For that individual, it may be more fun to be a spectator! If the guest list has been provided to you by the guest of honor and you are unsure of the personalities of the guests, be sure to ask her!

When choosing which games to play, make sure that you have all the necessary materials for the games, including several pens. Ensure that all pens are working especially if they are new. Too few pens or pens that are not working will slow down the party.

Games to Break the Ice

Thank You Cards

Provide precut pieces of paper folded in half to make a card for your guests. Have crayons spread around the table and have guests color a picture that is baby related. Make sure guests "sign" the back of their masterpiece. When everyone is done, gather the cards and have Mom-to-be choose a winner. These cards can then be used as thank you cards. Provide envelopes for guests to self-address so mom can mail them out more easily.

Baby Picture Match

On the invitation, request that each guest bring a baby picture of herself. Assemble the pictures on a board and assign each picture a number. Later in the shower, hand out a sheet of paper with the guests names to match with the baby pictures. The person with the most correct wins. If guests do not know each other well, nametags will help the process.

Variation: If your guests know each other well, you can add in pictures of babies from magazines or multiple pictures of some people.

Pay the Baby

This game requires a bank for the baby. For the guest's nametags, replace the name with a baby item. Throughout the shower, guests are referred to by their baby item. If someone uses the guests actual name, she must make a deposit into the baby's bank.

Did you?

Have guests find another guest who did unique things as a child. Examples are to look for someone who wore glasses, was born in another country, played a stringed instrument, was not born in a hospital, had a horse, was born the same month as the baby's due date, etc.

Design Baby's Clothes

Make a beautiful keepsake! Buy a few packages of baby t-shirts, onesies (one package of each size), or burp cloths and some fabric pens and/or paint. Each guest can draw, design, or write a well wish for the baby. Remember to place a piece of plastic or cardboard between the front and back sides of the clothing or your paint will seep through.

Get to Know Each Other

Pass around a roll of toilet paper, not explaining the rules of the game. Each guest takes what she thinks she will need. Then everyone counts her squares. Each person has to say one thing about herself for each square she has.

Words of Wisdom

Place several pieces of paper folded in a bowl. Each slip of paper has a number on it one through four. Each guest draws a slip of paper. The number on the slip represents how many pieces of advice she must share regarding child rearing.

Variation: Each piece of advice can be written on index cards and passed to the mom. She reads them and everyone guesses who gave which piece of advice.

Variation: A journal or the baby book can be set near the door and as people arrive, each person writes a piece of advice or well wish to the family.

Variation: Take a picture with Mom and each guest. Then have guests decorate a scrapbook page for their picture. They can include their bit of wisdom and advice on their page.

Baby Questions

Hand out cards and pencils to each guest. On each card is a common baby question, i.e. "What do you do when a baby cries?" After each guest has read her question, collect the cards and redistribute the cards face down to different people. On the back of the card, guests write the answer to the question they first read. They may write on the card, feed the baby but this time the question might say, "What do you do when baby is vomiting?" Recollect cards and read them aloud.

What's in a Name?

Prepare a list of all the guests' names. On the right side, list the meanings of each person's name. Guests match up the name with the correct meaning.

\

Games for the More Conservative Guests

Memory

Using a large piece of foam board, make 4 rows and 5 columns, so you have 20 squares. Keep the squares large, 3"x3", so everyone will be able to read the words. Fill each square with a pregnancy or baby related word. Cover each square with a piece of paper. Use poster gum to attach it. Poster gum allows the paper to be removed and reattached several times. Game is played like the children's game "Memory". When guests correctly make a match, they receive a candy bar that corresponds to the term they matched. Here are some examples: Babysitter = a real LIFESAVERs, Conception = SKOR, The father's name = SUGAR DADDY", or BIG HUNK, Laundry = MOUNDS are piling up, Family of 3 = 3 MUSKETEERS, Crunched for time = CRUNCH bar, Welcome baby = HERSHEY KISSES, Breastfeed = It's the MILKY WAY, Baby's playmate = BABY RUTH, Baby babble = M&M'S ("mamamamama"), Money = 100 GRAND.

Name the Baby Food

Purchase several jars of baby food. Number the bottom of each jar and place them upside down in a basket so the labels cannot be seen. Guests guess the variety of each jar. The most correct wins.

Who am I?

On separate cards, write the names of famous moms. Attach cards to the player's backs. Players have to guess whom they are by asking yes or no questions. The first one to correctly guess wins.

Guess My Birth Year and Weight

Hand out a sheet or paper with guest's names on it. Guests have to guess what year each person was born and what their birth weight was.

Poem

If the parents-to-be have picked a name, have guests offer a piece of advice beginning with each letter of the baby's name. For example:

Share your toys.
Hold your breath to get rid of hiccups.
Always give your mommy lots of hugs and kisses.
Yelling and screaming is a no-no.
Never pull mommy's hair.
Applesauce is good for you.

Cotton Ball Game

Blindfold each player. Place in front of them an empty bowl and a bowl full of cotton balls. With a spoon, players scoop the cotton balls from one bowl to the other. The one who puts the most into the empty bowl wins.

Baby Bingo

Divide a piece of paper into twenty-five squares and leave them blank. Write "Freebie" in the middle square. Before opening the gifts, hand out the sheets. Guests guess what gifts the mother-to-be will receive and fill in the squares with those items. The rules are the same as "Bingo". As the guest of honor opens her gifts, guests mark off the ones they have correct.

Find the Poopie Diaper

As each guest arrives, she receives a diaper to pin on her clothes. The diaper can be used as a nametag. After the gifts have been opened, each guest opens her diaper. The diaper with the poopie in it (a little smear of mustard) wins the door prize.

Fill in the Blank

Prepare a list of lullabies with missing words. Be sure to use lullabies that vary over many generations to make it a little more challenging. Guests fill in the blanks. The one with the most correct wins.

Guess the Girth

Each guest cuts a piece of ribbon the length that she believes is the circumference of the mom's tummy and writes her initials on it. The mommy wraps the ribbons around her tummy and the person who is the closest wins. This game can also be used with string or toilet paper.

Variation: The game can be played while gifts are being opened. As the mom opens a gift, the guest giving that gift comes up and receives a hug from the mom-to-be and tries to fit the ribbon around her tummy. This makes the gift opening more interactive.

Baby Animal Names

On a sheet of paper, list ten to fifteen baby animal names and a blank next to each name. Guests have to guess the adult name. Example: tadpole *frog*

Variation: To make the game a little harder, have guests guess the baby name instead of the adult name.

Mommy Quiz

Prepare ten silly questions about how the mom-to-be will respond to certain parenting situations. Give guests four possible answers. The guest with the most answers matching the mom-to-be wins.

Guess the Baby Food

Players are blindfolded and taste several different flavors of baby foods. Player who guesses the most correctly wins. To make the tasting more appealing, choose different fruit varieties.

Variation: Choose four guests and divide them into two teams. All four people are blindfolded. One person has to feed the other and whoever finishes their food first wins. Be sure to have bibs for the people being fed.

Variation: Instead of having guests taste the baby food, have them smell the different foods.

Grab Bags

Place one small baby item in each brown bag. Close bags and staple shut. Pass the bags around and guests have to guess what is in them. The most correct wins.

Variation: Spell out "baby shower" with the brown bags by writing one letter on each bag and have the item inside the bag begin with the letter written on it.

Name the Body Part

Make a list of about twenty objects that would be another name for a body part. Guests have to guess the body parts within one minute. The most correct wins. Some examples: Type of tree = palm, part of a clock = hands or face, a section of a relay = leg, the center of a storm = eye, building material = nails, a rabbit = hair, a burrowing animal = mole, a jerk = heel, a piece of corn = ear, a student = pupil

Variation: Use names instead of body parts. For example, money = Bill, early morning = Dawn

True or False

List several statements about the mother-to-be regarding her childhood and guests decide if the statements are true or false

Childhood

Find out details of the parents-to-be's childhoods. Who walked first, talked first, cried on the first day of school, etc. Have guests guess whether it was the mommy or the daddy. The most correct wins.

Timer Game

As the guest of honor is opening her gifts, set a timer. When the timer goes off, whoever gave the gift she is opening receives a prize. If you have a very talkative group, do not set the timer for too short of a time or you will give a prize for every gift.

Hospital Bag

This game will give the mom-to-be good suggestions to put in her bag if she has forgotten something. Place the mother-to-be's closed hospital bag on a table. Guests are told how many items are inside. Guests write down what they think is in the bag. The one with the most correct wins.

Word Search

Each player receives a sheet of paper that says "Shayna's Baby Shower" at the top. Guests have one minute to find as many words as possible. The one with the most words wins.

Variation: If the parents have picked out the baby's name, you can write his/her name at the top.

Baby Names

On a sheet of paper write the alphabet down the page. Guests have one minute to write down a baby name starting with each letter of the alphabet. For each name, players receive one point. For each original name that no one else has, players receive two points.

Baby Items

Give guests forty-five seconds to write down as many different baby items they can think of. Players get a point for each item written down that no one else wrote down. The one with the most points wins.

Name that Tune

Make a tape recording of several lullabies. Have guests guess the name of each lullaby.

Variation: Choose songs that have names in the title.

Variation: Choose songs that have the word "baby" in the title.

Variation: Choose nursery rhymes instead of songs.

Baby's Features

Blow up a color photo of the mother and father-to-be. Make several color copies of each. Hand each guest a set of pictures. Guests cut out and piece together a baby out of the facial parts. For large parties, you may opt to do this game in teams to keep the price down on the color copies.

The Price is Right

Purchase eight different baby items. Set them out in front of the guests. Each person has to guess the correct price of each item. The one who gets the closest without going over wins. Remember to save your receipt!

My Water Broke

Freeze plastic babies in ice cube trays and add them to your guest's drinks. The first one to melt has to yell, "My water broke!"

Variation: Freeze one baby in an ice cube tray. Each guest writes down what time the baby will be born (completely thawed from the ice cube). The person closest wins.

Hidden Safety Pins

Fill a bowl with rice and some small safety pins. Players are blindfolded and can only remove the safety pins from the bowl, not the rice. The person with the most pins wins. If you have a large party, you can play a few people at a time.

Paper Stork

Each guest receives an 8 1/2 X 11 sheet of construction paper. Players must tear out the shape of a stork with the paper behind her back. The guest with the paper most resembling a stork wins.

Don't Say Baby

Make necklaces out of thin ribbon and use safety pins or plastic baby items for charms. Each guest receives a necklace as she arrives to wear throughout the party. If a guest says the word "baby", she must turn her necklace over to the person who caught her saying it. The person with the most necklaces at the end of the party wins.

Draw a Baby

Each player receives a paper plate and a marker. They have to place the paper plate on their heads and draw a picture of a baby without looking.

Variation: After drawing the baby, everyone puts down his or her pen. Then they have to pick them up again and draw a diaper on the baby.

Mom and Dad

Put a few baby pictures of the mother and father-to-be at different ages on a board. Guests have to guess the ages.

Guess the Jelly Beans

Fill a baby bottle full of pink and/or blue jellybeans. Guests guess the number of beans. The one closest wins.

Word Scramble

Pass out sheets of paper with words relating to babies scrambled. Give the guests thirty seconds to unscramble the words.

Sticker Fun

If the party includes food, place a sticker on the bottom of one of the plates. After everyone is done eating, they look under the plate. The one with the sticker wins.

Variation: If food isn't being served, you can place a sticker under a chair.

Items on a Tray

Uncover a tray filled with several small baby items, such as, baby pins, travel size baby shampoo and oil, ear syringe, rattle, cotton balls, syrup of ipecac, socks, wash cloth, sippy cup, etc...Give guests thirty seconds to look at the tray. Cover it up again. The guest who can write down the most items wins. Of course, the mom to be receives the items.

Variation: After memorizing the items, have the guests answer questions relating to the baby items they saw. For example, Which Disney character is on the bib? What color is the sleeper?

Variation: Have a guest or the hostess hold the tray while everyone is looking. Then have her leave the room. Have the guests write down everything the person holding the tray was wearing.

Variation: Attach the items to a piece of rope. Stretch the rope out in front of the guests. Remove the rope and have them write down how long the rope was.

Variation: Place items in a box. Blindfold the players. Each player touches the items and then has to write down what they remember.

Diaper Door Prize

For every package of diapers a guest brings, her name is entered into a drawing held at the end of the shower.

Clothes Pin in a Jar

Each player stands over the top of a mason jar. She must drop the pin into the jar from the height of her nose. The most pins in wins.

Play-Doh Sculptures

Each guest receives a piece of play-doh to sculpt a specific baby item. This can be a timed event and the mother-to-be judges based on creativity and resemblance of the item.

Variation: You can use soft bubble gum to sculpt a baby or a baby item. The wrappers can be used for clothing or diapers.

Baby Product Logo

Gather several ads for different baby products. Cut out the brand name and put the ads on poster board. Number the ads from one to twenty and have guests guess which brand the ad is for. The one with the most correct wins.

Games for the More Adventurous Guests

Treasure Hunt

Hide baby items or small gifts around the house or where the shower is being held. Give guests a clue to lead to each item. In this game, people can hunt individually or in teams. If playing in teams, one team can be called early, one called late, and one called on time. The team that wins determines the "birth-date". Teams can also be called boy and girl to determine baby's sex.

Baby Pictionary

Divide guests into two teams. The first artist draws a phrase out of a bowl. All phrases are baby related. Both teams have a chance to guess. The team that guesses correctly earns five points for the team. Teams alternate drawing. Here are some ideas for your phrases: dirty diapers, midnight feedings, delivery room, maternity clothes, potty training, ob/gyn, circumcision, newborn, first word, high chair, breast pump, diaper bag, changing table, labor, hospital bag, ultrasound, breathe, nightgown, onesies, sponge bath, umbilical cord, diaper rash, stretch marks, sleepless nights, joy, rocking chair, grandmother, stuffed animals, receiving blanket, womb.

Delivery

This game must be played outdoors. Carefully put a small, plastic baby in a balloon. Fill the balloon with water and tie it on a string. Players have to tie the balloon around their waists and squat over an upturned nail (drive a nail through a piece of wood). The first one to deliver the baby wins.

Baby Relay

Divide guests into teams. Teammates decide amongst themselves which part of the relay to do. The first person has to be fed baby food, then drink a small amount of liquid from a bottle. The next person diapers a doll and then runs it to the next person. The next person rocks the baby and sings Rock-a-bye Baby in its entirety. The team that finishes first wins.

What's in a Baby's Room?

This game starts with the mommy-to-be. She throws a stuffed animal to a guest. Upon catching it, the guest must say something that is in a baby's room. If she can't think of anything or if an item was repeated, that person is out. The person left is the winner.

What's in the Diaper?

This game is not for people with weak stomachs! Get five diapers and five different candy bars. Melt half of the candy in the microwave on wax paper. Smear the candy inside the diaper and mark the diaper with a number. Do this the day before the shower. During the game, pass the diapers and give guests five minutes to figure out what is in the diaper.

Pass the Baby

This game is played like musical chairs. When the music plays, you pass the baby. When it stops, the person holding the baby is out of the game. The winner is the last one left not holding the baby.

Diaper Changing Contest

Each player has a plastic baby doll in a "dirty" diaper. When the timer goes off, each player has to remove the dirty diaper, which is full of yellow mustard, clean the baby, and rediaper it in a cloth diaper, pinned on. The fastest one wins.

Variation: Blindfold each player. A stuffed animal and a diaper is laying within five feet in front of the player. Player has twenty seconds to find the animal and diaper it.

Variation: Players have to diaper and dress the baby.

Variation: Divide guests into four teams. Each team has one minute to diaper one of the teammates.

Pin the Diaper on the Baby

Make a big picture of a baby with an outline of where the diaper should go. Make several copies of diapers in blue and/or pink papers. Use the same rules as "Pin the Tail on the Donkey"

A Typical Day

Each participant has to go through a "typical" day as a Mom. Answer the phone and while talking she must change the baby's diaper, hang diapers on the line, etc. The player with the fastest time wins.

PRIZES

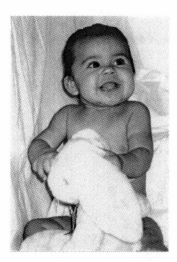

Kaylee Michele
8 months

I prayed for this child, and
the Lord has granted me
what I asked of him.

1 Samuel 1:27

It is customary to give a small prize for the winner of each game. Prizes do not have to be expensive or elaborate. Use your imagination.

Some hosts prefer to give something for everyone who participates in a game. This is a good alternative to giving party favors. However, that decision is up to the person giving the shower. If you choose to give to everyone, why not give a gift that compliments the winner's gift? The ideas are endless. Here are some gift ideas for just the winner and gift ideas for everyone.

- ❖ Candy
  - ◦ Give a box of chocolates and then pass a box of chocolates around and each person chooses a piece.

- ❖ Candles
  - ◦ Give the winner a nice candle and everyone else receives a potpourri sachet.

- ❖ Vase
  - ◦ Fill a small vase with candy and everyone else receives a few pieces of candy.

- ❖ Bath Products
  - ◦ Give a gift basket filled with bath products and everyone else receives a little sachet of sea salts or bath pearls.

- ❖ Stationary
  - ◦ Give a set of stationary and to everyone else a cute pencil.

- ❖ Homemade Breads or Desserts
  - ◦ Give a basket full of homemade goodies like cookies or muffins, and everyone else gets a cookie.

- ❖ Gift Baskets
  - ◦ Make a gift basket for the winner filled with garden hand tools, gloves, and seeds in a terra cotta pot. Everyone receives a package of flower seeds.

  - ◦ Make a basket with cookie cutters, cookie dough, and a spatula in a mixing bowl and everyone receives a cookie cutter.

❖ Book
  ◦ Give a book and to everyone else bookmarks.

❖ Coffee Mug
  ◦ Fill a large coffee mug with various teas and hand out a bag of tea to everyone.

❖ Candlesticks
  ◦ To the winner the candlesticks and to everyone else a small votive candle.

❖ Frames
  ◦ Choose a frame for the winner and for everyone else a small magnetic frame.

❖ Potpurri
  ◦ Give a bowl or vase filled with potpourri and everyone else receives a sachet.

❖ Small Gift Certificates for Local Stores or Restaurants
  ◦ When you purchase the gift certificate, ask the restaurant if they have coupons for discounted meals and give those to everyone else.

❖ Pastel Pens and Pencils Tied with Ribbon
  ◦ Make a "bouquet" with pens and pencils and everyone else receives an eraser.

❖ Flowers
  ◦ Give a bouquet or vase filled with flowers and a sachet of potpourri to everyone else.

❖ Handmade Items

FAVORS

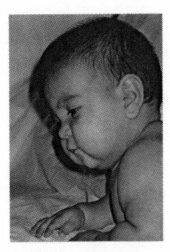

Layna Alexandra
6 months

Party favors are a nice way to say thank you to your guests for coming to the shower. If you know that the mother-to-be is not one to be quick with thank you cards, attach a cute note or poem to the favor. This will help to alleviate some of the pressure mothers feel. Favors can also be used as part of your decorations. They can be used as place cards, centerpieces, or table decorations. Many of the party favors listed below can be used with the different themes and decors in the previous chapters.

Let the children come to me,
and do not hinder them, for
the kingdom of heaven
belongs to such as these.

Matthew 19:14

❖   Fill a small clay pot, paper maché box, or teacup with seeds, flowers, herbs, candy, or a flower bulb.

❖   Wrap a votive candle in tissue paper or pieces of a receiving blanket tied with ribbon and a baby charm.

❖   Make something homemade like jam or muffins.

❖   Make chocolate candies using candy molds that suit your theme or décor.

❖   Buy or make glycerin soaps. If you make them, insert a small baby item so it "floats" in the soap.

❖   Make potpourri filled sachets.

❖   Give bookmarks that match the theme.

❖   Take a picture with the mother-to-be and each guest. Slip the picture into a frame and send it home with your guests.

❖   If the majority of your guests have small kids, for fun, give a rubber ducky or bubbles!

❖   Make bags filled with candies having baby related names like Sugar Babies, Hugs, Kisses, Almond Joy, and Baby Ruth. Tie it with ribbon and attach a small baby charm.

❖   Make magnets. Purchase magnet sheets that have adhesive on one side or hot glue a small magnet onto the back of a picture that you have taken of the mother-to-be and each guest. Or attach a magnet to something that is related to the theme or décor of the party.

❖ Buy plain white potholders and decorate them with fabric paints. Write the mother-to-be's name and the date of the shower.

❖ Make chocolate covered pretzels sprinkled with blue or pink sugar or nonpareils. Tie three or five pretzels together with matching ribbon.

❖ Offer the flower centerpieces as favors.

❖ Fill baby food jars with pastel M & M's. Tie a ribbon around the neck of the jar.

❖ Give cookie cutters in the shape of baby items or something related to the theme or décor of the shower.

❖ Make cinnamon rolls. Wrap in plastic wrap and tie with blue or pink ribbon. Attach a note saying "Thank you for celebrating 'Shayna's' bun in the oven."

❖ Find cookie sheets that have a place to insert a stick and make lollipop cookie bouquets.

POEMS

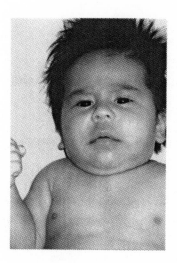

Poems can be used to include on thank you notes attached to favors, place cards, or just printed nicely and framed as decorations. These poems were written by unknown authors. Enjoy!

Daniel Ray
2 months

And he took the children in his arms, put his hands on them and blessed them.

Mark 10:16

I'm sorry I couldn't be with you but I'm terribly busy you see
Painting my eyes, my cheeks, my hair so my parents will be proud of me.
I'm sending this little message to convey to you this thought,
God will soon have sent me to use the gifts you brought.
Thanks for the lovely welcome you have given me today,
And when you see the stars in the sky you'll know I've come to stay.
Be sure to come and see me as soon as I get here.
Just give my mother lots of time to dress me up my dear.

Love,
Baby

Sorry I can't be with you to share in Mommy's shower
But you see I'm very busy 'cause I'm growing more each hour.
I'll be arriving shortly I'm as happy as can be
So after I've been home awhile please come and visit me!

Love,
Baby

We'd like to thank you for making this fuss,
And for coming over to hang around with us.
My name is _____ and I'll be here real soon
Then I can hang with you from morning until noon.
I'm a little busy, to say the least
But we're glad you hung around to enjoy the feast.
Thank you for the gift, it'll come in real handy.
No matter what it is, it will work just dandy.
This little gift is for you,
To help you remember you see,
To come back and hang around some more with Mommy and me.

Love,
Baby

This is a gift for you today
So when I'm born you'll light my way.
And when that happy day is here,
Burn this candle and spread good cheer.

Love,
Baby

Sent From Above

This tiny little baby was sent from God above
To fill our hearts with happiness
And light our lives with love.

Little Hands

My little hands play patty-cake
they peek-a-boo and wave...
They catch me while I learn to walk
and splash me as I bathe.

My little hands reach up to you
for hugs before I sleep...
And fold together when I pray
the Lord my soul to keep.

My little hands are tiny now
but yours will serve to guide me...
And when I'm grown I'll still reach out
and know you're right beside me.

Someday…

Someday I'll jump through puddles,
take a stroll or run a race.
Someday I'll walk across the street
or maybe walk in space.
Someday I'll scale a mountain
or I'll join a ballet corps.
Someday I'll walk a tightrope
or explore the ocean floor.
Someday these feet will do some things
that only heaven knows,
but for today they're happy
just to wiggle all their toes.

Love Stronger

A baby is a small person that makes love stronger,
days shorter, nights longer,
the home happier,
the clothes shabbier,
the past forgotten,
the future worth living for.

Sunshine

She's a little bit of sunshine,
She's a smile to light your days,
She will steal your heart and
keep it with her warm endearing ways,
She's your precious little daughter,
With a sweetness from above
Who will fill your years with laughter
and your lives with lots of love.

Tonight

You and I
will never be this close again.
By morning
you will be a tiny person
all your own.
No longer the kicking, demanding
bulge in my body
that I have grown to love so well.

I pray God will safely guide you
on your journey tonight,
and I ask Him for the strength
to help you all I can.

Again you signal
your impatience to be free.
Time to wake your daddy.

Precious Baby

Nothing more precious to keep,
In tones of a hue so deep,
As soft as a silent prayer,
A lock of my baby's hair.

Our Prayer

We prayed a long time
Asking God for you.
We shared our dreams
And cried to Him, too.

He listened and answered
Our prayerful plea,
And that's when He gave you
to your dad and me!

Blessed

Blessings on the little children,
Sweet and fresh from Heaven above,
May their days be filled with beauty,
May they grow in truth and love.
Lord, bless this tiny infant
Who will make the world so fair
Keep this precious little life
Forever in Your care.

The Creator

God made the world with its towering trees,
majestic mountains and restless seas,
Then stopped and said, "It needs one more thing…
someone to laugh and dance and sing,
To walk in the woods and gather flowers,
to commune with Me in quiet hours."
So God created little girls,
with laughing eyes and bouncing curls,
With joyful hearts and infectious smiles,
And when He'd completed the task He'd begun,
He was pleased and proud of the job He'd done.
For the world, when seen through a little girl's eyes,
Greatly resembles Paradise.

A Gift

Ten little fingers,
Ten tiny toes,
The sweetest of smiles
And a cute little nose.
All these add up
To a very special
thing—A BABY
The greatest of gifts
That life can bring

Perfection

Tiny fingers, tiny toes
Little itty, bitty clothes
Teddy bears and smiles of joy
Will it be a girl or boy?

Chosen One

Chosen One—Welcome Home
Tonight as you lie sleeping
for the first time in your bed
There must be something lasting
and profound that should be said!

But as your face is gazed upon
framed by dark, raven hair
No words can tell or quite express
the feelings that we share.

The wait is finally over.
You're home at last to stay.
And there'll always be the memories
of the joy that's filled this day!

With love that's brimming over
by the sight of you alone
Welcome home, dear cherished one
at long last…Welcome Home!

One Hope

One sought for you a home that she could not provide—
The other prayed for a child and her hope was not denied.

Wishing

We made a wish
And it came true,
We made a wish
and God sent you.

Our Joy

He's our morning's first smile,
our bundle of hugs,
a heart full of wonder and joy.
He's everything precious
and cuddly and sweet
He's our wonderful baby boy.

Treasure the Day

At first you didn't lift your head;
You didn't know to smile.
The time before you knew my voice
Seemed such a long, long while.
I couldn't wait for you to roll,
And then to sit and clap.
And now you're off and crawling,
Not helpless in my lap.
Why didn't someone tell me
How fast a baby grows,
That every little baby stage
Soon comes, but sooner goes.

So I'll enjoy the fleeting time
Before you learn to walk.
And treasure every tiny noise
Before you learn to talk.
For soon you'll learn to walk,
Then run,
And talk and sing a song,
And never be my babe again.
The babe's forever gone.

One

Little baby, take your time,
For while you are tiny, you are mine.
For these precious nine months,
We're together as one.
Our hearts beat in tandem,
A Mother and Son.

My Baby, Unborn

Blessings upon you,
my baby unborn.
Safely inside me,
asleep and so warm.
Sleep must come easy,
to those who are unborn.
As the Maker so silently,
fashions your form.

Tomorrow

Tomorrow's child small and warm,
Tiny hands reach up to touch and prod,
Small toes stretch and something deep inside
Feels like the ripple of a giggle,
As our tiny precious unborn child begins to laugh…and dance…and wiggle.

EATING FOR TWO

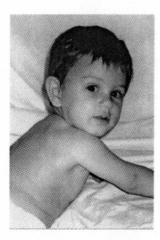

Marley Jakob
7 months

They are the children
God has graciously given
your servant.

Genesis 33:5

As host of the shower, it is obvious you have a love for the mother-to-be. Remind her that you are available to help her throughout the remainder of her pregnancy.

Many pregnant women do not attend childbirth classes and if they do, it is very late in their pregnancies. It goes without saying that nutrition is a priority and the sooner she is aware of the special needs of her body, the healthier she and the baby will be. Below is a list of the different foods she must include in her diet and the benefits of those foods.

❖   At least 2 servings of fish, chicken, beef, beans or other source of complete proteins daily. Adequate protein prevents fatigue and a lack of appetite. Consuming a minimum of 100 grams of protein will help guard her against a dangerous condition called toxemia which can threaten the life of her and her baby.

❖   4 glasses of milk (or the equivalent) daily. Calcium and other minerals and vitamins found in dairy products will help relieve insomnia and muscle cramps. It is also good for the strength of her muscles and bones.

❖   3 servings of whole wheat bread and/ or whole grain cereal daily. Whole grain breads and cereals are high in carbohydrates which are fuel to your body. Whole grains are also an excellent source of B vitamins, which aid in the normal functioning of nerve tissue.

❖   1 piece of citrus fruit (or the equivalent) daily. Citrus is high in vitamin C which assists in iron absorption and fighting disease. It also helps your skin to stretch and stay strong. Deficiency in vitamin C can weaken your uterus and not allow it to function properly.

❖   2 servings of green vegetables daily. Dark green vegetables are high in vitamin A and B complex. These vitamins help assimilate the protein found in other foods. It is also rich in folic acid. The darker the green the higher in vitamins and minerals.

❖   1 serving a day of yellow and orange fruits and vegetables. Yellow and orange colored fruits and vegetables are a great source of vitamin A. Vitamin A also aids in fighting infection.

❖ 1 serving of other fruits and vegetables. Eating a variety of fruits and vegetables ensures that she receives all the necessary vitamins and minerals.

❖ 4 cups of water per 50 pounds of body weight daily. Remember that caffeine beverages, juice, or teas do not take the place of water. She must still have the recommended amount of water above any other beverages she is drinking. Dehydration will drain energy and can also cause headaches.

❖ Salt food to taste to increase blood volume.

❖ 3 servings of fats daily. That includes butter and oils used in cooking. Fats also help your skin to stretch and it is also a source of energy should her body need it. Fats are necessary for the proper neurological development of the baby.

HOSPITAL CHECKLIST

With all of the changes in the mother-to-be's life, it is easy for her to forget some of those special items that she may want to bring with her to the hospital. Make sure she has a checklist so she is as comfortable as possible. Also, find out her wishes while she is at the hospital. She may or may not be comfortable with visitors. At the shower, make these requests known to guests who seem interested in visiting.

Jovanna Danielle
16 months

From the lips of children
and infants you have
ordained praise.

Psalms 8:2

For the Mother & Father:

_____Nightgown
_____Light Bathrobe
_____Slippers
_____Nursing Bra
_____Socks
_____Ponytail Holder
_____Deck of Cards
_____Chapstick
_____Toiletries
_____Chux Pads
_____Clothes to Go Home In
_____Camera & Film
_____Video Camera
_____Music
_____Watch to Time Contractions
_____List of Phone Numbers
_____Pillow

For the Baby:

_____Clothes to Wear Home
_____Car Seat
_____Gown / Undershirts
_____Receiving Blankets
_____Diapers
_____Baby Book

FINAL THOUGHT

"For I know the plans I have for you," declares the Lord, "plans to prosper you and not to harm you, plans to give you a hope and a future. Then you will call upon me and come and pray to me, and I will listen to you. You will seek me and find me when you seek me with all your heart. I will be found by you," declares the Lord. Jeremiah 29:11-14.

The Lord has big plans for you! If you have been uncertain of your destiny or not sure what the ultimate purpose was in your life, now is the time to know. He wants to give you a life of fulfillment and peace. God wants to restore your relationships, your finances and your health. He wants to heal your marriage and your relationships with your children. But he cannot move in your life until you receive Jesus.

If you have never accepted Jesus as your personal Lord and Savior, he is waiting for you. If you confess with your mouth, "Jesus is Lord," and believe in your heart that God raised him from the dead, you will be saved. For it is with your heart that you believe and are justified, and it is with your mouth that you confess and are saved. Romans 10:9,10.

Wherever you are, pray this and receive Jesus in your life. Say, "Lord Jesus, I need You in my life. I believe You are the Son of God and that You died on the cross for me. Please forgive me of my sins and create a clean heart in me. Renew my spirit so that I can hear Your voice. I accept You as my Savior! You are my Lord!"

You now have a new life! A life of hope and a future. Now when you pray, God is listening. You will find him when you seek him. He wants to be with you. He loves you. You are his child.

If you have said this prayer and would like more information about what has just happened in your life, please log on to www.cotw.org. Send Pastors Dan and Laura an email and let them know about this awesome event in your life! They will be able to guide you and give you information on what is ahead for you. God bless you!

ABOUT THE AUTHOR

Shayna Andrews has committed her life to serving the Lord, Jesus Christ. She has a heart to minister to the needs of pregnant women and see the Lord transform women's lives and relationships. She has a blessed marriage of 7 years and is a mother to a beautiful, 3 year old daughter and is awaiting God to fulfill the promise of a baby boy. She and her family currently reside in Phoenix, Arizona.